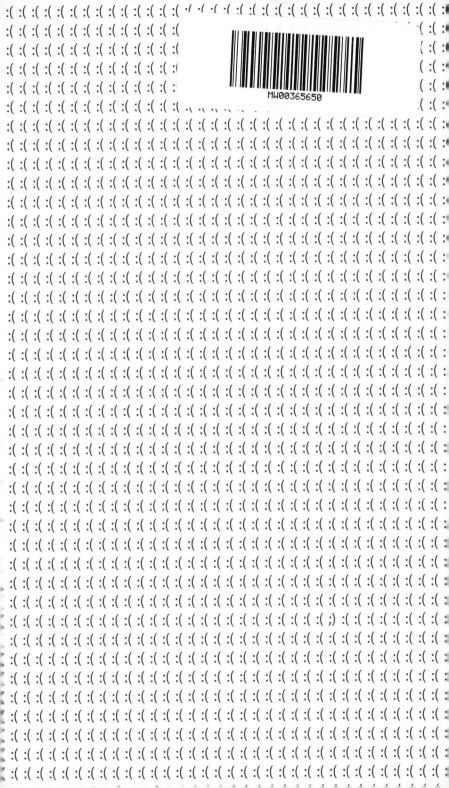

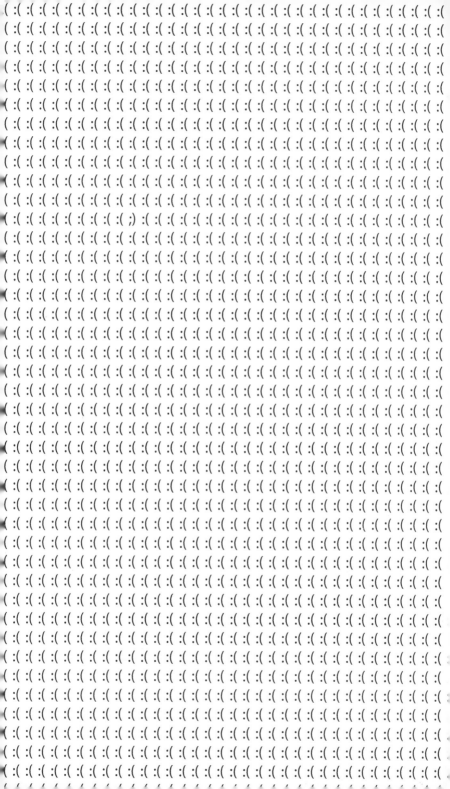

Perpetual Disappointments Diary

Nick Asbury

PICADOR

First published 2014 by Asbury & Asbury

First published 2016 by Boxtree

This updated edition published 2020 by Picador
an imprint of Pan Macmillan
The Smithson, 6 Briset Street, London EC1M 5NR
EU representative: Macmillan Publishers Ireland Ltd, 1st Floor,
The Liffey Trust Centre, 117–126 Sheriff Street Upper, Dublin 1, D01 YC43
Associated companies throughout the world
www.panmacmillan.com

ISBN 978-1-5290-3865-1

'Bank Insecurity Questions' first published by *McSweeney's Internet Tendency*.

Thanks to Jim Sutherland and everyone who has helped
make this diary what it unfortunately is.

9 8 7 6 5 4 3 2

A CIP catalogue record for this book is available from the British Library.

Printed in China.

Instructions

1.

2.

3.

4.

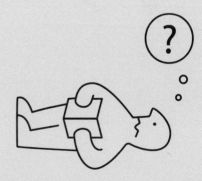

- This diary is suitable for use any year – it doesn't matter.
- Write a 'M' for Monday on the first Monday of the year, then count seven days forward and write another 'M'.
- Skip 29 February if it's not a leap year. Do not mess this one up.

Personal Information

Name

Address

Telephone

Mobile

Email

Previous Convictions

Known Medical Conditions

Next Of Kin

Bin Night

If this diary has been lost, on no account start an inspirational social media campaign to find its owner.

Bank Insecurity Questions

Which parts of your body are you most uncomfortable with?

When you chose that outfit this morning, how did you think you looked?

How does it feel watching your friends become successful?

On a scale of 1 to 10, how much does your birth father look like you?

Could a stranger theoretically have a copy of your front door key?

Are you sure about your answers so far?

What do you think your partner says to other people about your sex life?

Do you ever wonder what people think of your speaking voice?

Do the rumours going round lately concern you?

Why do dogs look at you like that?

Conversion Factors

Length

1 millimetre (mm)		0.0394 in
1 centimetre (cm)	10 mm	0.3937 in
1 metre (m)	100 cm	1.0936 yd
1 kilometre (km)	1 000 m	0.6214 mile
1 miss		1 mile

Area

1 sq cm (cm²)	100 mm²	0.1550 in²
1 sq metre (m²)	10 000 cm²	1.1960 yd²
1 sq kilometre (km²)	100 hectares	0.3861 mile²
1 sq meal (ml²)		1 Pot Noodle

Mass

1 milligram (mg)		0.0154 grain
1 gram (g)	1 000 mg	0.0353 oz
1 metric carat	0.2 g	3.0865 grains
1 kilogram (kg)	1 000 g	2.2046 lb
1 tonne (t)	1 000 kg	0.9842 ton
1 damp squib		0.1345 lead balloon

Capacity

1 litre (l)	1 dm³	1.76 pt
1 hectolitre (hl)	100 l	21.998 gal
1 glass		½ empty

Temperature °C	°F	Description
100	212	scalding
40	104	cup-a-soup
39	102.2	worrying fever
30	86	dreaded sunny day
21	70	room temperature
10	50	bedsit temperature
0	32	brass monkeys
-1	30.2	frosty glance
-18	0	icy stare
-40	-40	cold day in hell

Length

1 inch (in)		2.54 cm
1 foot (ft)	12 in	0.3048 m
1 yard (yd)	3 ft	0.9144 m
1 mile	1 760 yd	1.6093 km
1 stare	1 000 yd	0.9144 km

Area

1 sq inch (in^2)		6.4516 cm^2
1 sq foot (ft^2)	144 in^2	0.0929 m^2
1 sq yard (yd^2)	9 ft^2	0.8361 m^2
1 acre	4 840 yd^2	4 046.9 m^2
1 sq mile (mile^2)	640 acres	2.590 km^2
1 sq peg (peg^2)		1 round hole

Mass

1 ounce (oz)	437.5 grains	28.35 g
1 pound (lb)	16 oz	0.4536 kg
1 stone	14 lb	6.3503 kg
1 hundredweight (cwt)	112 lb	50.802 kg
1 ton	20 cwt	1.016 t
1 deadweight	1 millstone	0.5 albatross

Capacity

1 fluid ounce (fl oz)		28.413 ml
1 pint (pt)	20 fl oz	0.5683 l
1 gallon (gal)	8 pt	4.546 l
1 Kestrel Super (pt)		9.0% vol

Useful Phrases
English, French, German, Spanish and Mandarin

I have lost my passport

F: J'ai perdu mon passeport

G: Ich habe meinen Pass verloren

S: He perdido el pasaporte

M: 我丢了护照

I am on the wrong plane

F: Je me suis trompé d'avion

G: Ich bin im falschen Flugzeug

S: Me he equivocado de avión

M: 我上错了飞机

I have destroyed my hire car

F: J'ai accidenté ma voiture de location

G: Ich habe mein Mietauto kaputt gefahren

S: He estrellado el coche de alquiler

M: 我毁掉了租来的车子

I do not have health insurance

F: Je n'ai pas d'assurance maladie

G: Ich habe keine Krankenversicherung

S: No tengo seguro médico

M: 我没有医疗保险

When will the construction work finish?

F: Quand est-ce que les travaux de construction seront-ils finis?

G: Wann sind die Bauarbeiten vorbei?

S: ¿Cuando acabarán las obras?

M: 这工程什么时候竣工?

Can I book an alarm call for midday?

F: Puis-je vous demander de me reveiller à midi?

G: Kann ich bitte einen Weckanruf für mittags buchen?

S: Necesito que me despierten a mediodía

M: 我想订一个中午叫起服务?

A table for one, please

F: Une table pour une personne, s'il vous plaît

G: Einen Tisch für eine Person, bitte

S: Mesa para uno, por favor

M: 一位

What meat is this?

F: Quel type de viande est-ce?

G: Was für ein Fleisch is das?

S: ¿De qué es esta carne?

M: 这是什么肉?

Do you have any very cheap wine?

F: Avez-vous un vin vraiment bon marché?

G: Haben Sie irgendeinen sehr billigen Wein?

S: ¿Tienen algún vino barato?

M: 有没有便宜的酒

Same again, please

F: La même chose, s'il vous plaît

G: Das Gleiche nochmal bitte

S: Más de lo mismo, por favor

M: 再来一样的, 谢谢

I am sorry I spilt your drink

F: Excusez-moi d'avoir renversé votre boisson

G: Tut mir leid, dass ich Ihr Getränk verschüttet habe

S: Siento haberle tirado la bebida

M: 对不起我打翻了你的杯子

Anywhere. Just drive.

F: N'importe où. Vous n'avez qu'à conduire.

G: Egal wohin. Fahren Sie einfach.

S: A donde sea. Limítese a conducir.

M: 开车－去哪儿都好

Watch out for that truck!

F: Faites attention à ce poids lourd!

G: Vorsichtig, passen Sie auf den Lastwagen auf!

S: ¡Cuidado con ese camión!

M: 小心那货车!

I apologise, officer

F: Je m'excuse, monsieur l'agent

G: Es tut mir sehr leid, Herr Polizist

S: Le pido disculpas, agente

M: 对不起, 长官

I would like to reverse the charges

F: Veuillez demander à mon correspondant de payer la communication

G: Ich möchte bitte ein R-Gespräch anmelden

S: Me gustaría hacer una llamada a cobro revertido

M: 我想打一通受话人付费电话

I am locked in the toilet

F: Je me suis enfermé(e) dans les toilettes

G: Ich bin in der Toilette eingeschlossen

S: Estoy atrapado/atrapada en el baño

M: 我被困在厕所里

I have run out of petrol

F: Je n'ai plus de carburant

G: Mein Tank ist alle

S: Me he quedado sin gasolina

M: 我没汽油了

Police, fire and ambulance please

F: S'il vous plaît, envoyez la police, les pompiers et une ambulance

G: Polizei, Feuerwehr und Rettungswagen, bitte

S: Mande a la policía, los bomberos y una ambulancia, por favor

M: 我想叫警察, 消防车跟救护车

Not guilty

F: Non coupable

G: Nicht schuldig

S: Inocente

M: 不认罪

Can you stop talking?

F: Pouvez-vous arrêter de parler?

G: Können Sie bitte aufhören zu reden?

S: ¿Quiere hacer el favor de callarse?

M: 你可以闭嘴吗?

You might want to give it ten minutes

F: Je vous conseille d'attendre dix minutes

G: Ich würde da erstmal nicht reingehen

S: Quizás debería esperar diez minutos

M: 你要等它十分钟

I am tired

F: Je suis fatigué(e)

G: Ich bin müde

S: Estoy agotado/agotada

M: 我很累

It doesn't matter

F: Ne vous en faites pas

G: Ist total egal

S: No importa

M: 没关系了

Notable Deaths

Hank Williams
1 January 1953

Townes Van Zandt
1 January 1997

Derek Acorah
3 January 2020

Amelia Earhart
5 January 1939

David Bowie
10 January 2016

James Joyce
13 January 1941

Cyrille Regis
14 January 2018

Shep
17 January 1987

Audrey Hepburn
20 January 1993

Terry Jones
21 January 2020

Mark E. Smith
24 January 2018

Kobe Bryant
26 January 2020

Pete Seeger
27 January 2014

A.A. Milne
31 January 1956

Buddy Holly
3 February 1959

Alexander Pushkin
10 February 1837

Sylvia Plath
11 February 1963

Harper Lee
19 February 2016

Duncan Edwards
21 February 1958

Stan Laurel
23 February 1965

Stanley Matthews
23 February 2000

Donald Bradman
25 February 2001

Georges Perec
3 March 1982

Ivor Cutler
3 March 2006

John Candy
4 March 1994

Mark Linkous
6 March 2010

Ken Dodd
11 March 2018

Karl Marx
14 March 1883

Jim Bowen
14 March 2018

Stephen Hawking
14 March 2018

Chuck Berry
18 March 2017

Arthur C. Clarke
19 March 2008

Johann Wolfgang
von Goethe
22 March 1832

Johan Cruyff
24 March 2016

Garry Shandling
24 March 2016

Ian Dury
27 March 2000

Virginia Woolf
28 March 1941

Isaac Newton
31 March 1727

Jesse Owens
31 March 1980

Kurt Cobain
5 April 1994

P.T. Barnum
7 April 1891

Frank Mars
8 April 1934

Pablo Picasso
8 April 1973

Edward Thomas
9 April 1917

Robert Edwards
10 April 2013

Franklin D. Roosevelt
12 April 1945

Thomas Andrews
15 April 1912

Greta Garbo
15 April 1990

Gabriel García Márquez
17 April 2014

Albert Einstein
18 April 1955

Anne Williams
18 April 2013

Charles Darwin
19 April 1882

Levon Helm
19 April 2012

Rubin Carter
20 April 2014

Prince Rogers Nelson
21 April 2016

Saul Bass
25 April 1996

Charley Patton
28 April 1934

Casey Jones
30 April 1900

Ayrton Senna
1 May 1994

Leonardo da Vinci
2 May 1519

Adam Yauch
4 May 2012

Henry David Thoreau
6 May 1862

Maurice Sendak
8 May 2012

Bob Marley
11 May 1981

Douglas Adams
11 May 2001

Doris Day
13 May 2019

Frank Sinatra
14 May 1998

June Carter Cash
15 May 2003

Ian Curtis
18 May 1980

Bonnie Parker
23 May 1934

Roger Moore
23 May 2017

Samuel Pepys
26 May 1703

Eric Morecambe
28 May 1984

John Noakes
28 May 2017

Christopher Marlowe
30 May 1593

Muhammad Ali
3 June 2016

David Markson
4 June 2010

Ray Bradbury
5 June 2012

Alan Turing
7 June 1954

Dorothy Parker
7 June 1967

Gerard Manley
Hopkins
8 June 1889

Hovis Presley
9 June 2005

Les Dawson
10 June 1993

Ella Fitzgerald
15 June 1996

James Gandolfini
19 June 2013

Niccolò Machiavelli
21 June 1527

Judy Garland
22 June 1969

Michael Jackson
25 June 2009

Tove Jansson
27 June 2001

Marlon Brando
1 July 2004

Ernest Hemingway
2 July 1961

Caroline Aherne
2 July 2016

Marie Curie
4 July 1934

Aneurin Bevan
6 July 1960

Notable Deaths (cont)

Billie Holiday
17 July 1959

John Coltrane
17 July 1967

Caravaggio
18 July 1610

Alan Lomax
19 July 2002

Amy Winehouse
23 July 2011

Samuel Taylor
Coleridge
25 July 1834

Vincent van Gogh
29 July 1890

Bobby Robson
31 July 2009

Cilla Black
1 August 2015

Joseph Conrad
3 August 1924

Lenny Bruce
3 August 1966

Marilyn Monroe
5 August 1962

Barry Chuckle
5 August 2018

Francis Ponge
6 August 1988

Tony Wilson
10 August 2007

Robin Williams
11 August 2014

William Blake
12 August 1827

Robert Johnson
16 August 1938

Aretha Franklin
16 August 2018

Bruce Forsyth
18 August 2017

Federico García Lorca
19 August 1936

Groucho Marx
19 August 1977

Jerry Lewis
20 August 2017

Neil Armstrong
25 August 2012

John McCain
25 August 2018

Gene Wilder
29 August 2016

Seamus Heaney
30 August 2013

J. R. R. Tolkien
2 September 1973

Steve Irwin
4 September 2006

Joan Rivers
4 September 2014

Roko Camaj
11 September 2001

Johnny Cash
12 September 2003

Grace Kelly
14 September 1982

Isambard Kingdom
Brunel
15 September 1859

Jimi Hendrix
18 September 1970

Virgil
21 September 19BC

Alan Fletcher
21 September 2006

Herman Melville
28 September 1891

Bill Shankly
29 September 1981

James Dean
30 September 1955

Woody Guthrie
3 October 1967

Tom Petty
2 October 2017

Peter Norman
3 October 2006

Janis Joplin
4 October 1970

Steve Jobs
5 October 2011

Jack Daniel
10 October 1911

Orson Welles
10 October 1985

Sean Hughes
16 October 2017

Thomas Edison
18 October 1931

Jack Kerouac
21 October 1969

Rosa Parks
24 October 2005

Fats Domino
24 October 2017

Geoffrey Chaucer
25 October 1400

John Peel
25 October 2004

Lou Reed
27 October 2013

Ted Hughes
28 October 1998

Ezra Pound
1 November 1972

Ernst Gombrich
3 November 2001

Jacques Tati
5 November 1982

Steve McQueen
7 November 1980

Leonard Cohen
7 November 2016

John Milton
8 November 1674

Arthur Rimbaud
10 November 1891

George Edwin Ellison
11 November 1918

John F. Kennedy
22 November 1963

Clive James
24 November 2019

Horace
27 November 8BC

George Harrison
29 November 2001

Oscar Wilde
30 November 1900

Odetta
2 December 2008

Frank Zappa
4 December 1993

Bob Willis
4 December 2019

Wolfgang Amadeus
Mozart
5 December 1791

Nelson Mandela
5 December 2013

John Lennon
8 December 1980

Patrick Moore
9 December 2012

Otis Redding
10 December 1967

Richard Pryor
10 December 2005

Sam Cooke
11 December 1964

Keith Chegwin
11 December 2017

Walt Disney
15 December 1966

Kirsty MacColl
18 December 2000

John Steinbeck
20 December 1968

Joe Strummer
22 December 2002

William Thackeray
24 December 1863

Charlie Chaplin
25 December 1977

Dean Martin
25 December 1995

George Michael
25 December 2016

Carrie Fisher
27 December 2016

Debbie Reynolds
28 December 2016

Bob Monkhouse
29 December 2003

On This Day

Leonardo da Vinci unsuccessfully tests flying machine
3 January 1496

First automobile hearse in use
15 January 1909

Black Monday
21 January 2008

Edvard Munch inspired to paint *The Scream*
22 January 1892

First canned beer sold
24 January 1935

Visitor falls down stairs in Fitzwilliam Museum, Cambridge, breaking three Qing Dynasty Chinese vases
25 January 2006

First electric dental drill
26 January 1875

Facebook founded
4 February 2004

First doughnut-making machine
6 February 1926

Longest traffic jam on record (109 miles)
16 February 1980

Opening and closing night of *Moose Murders*, worst-performing Broadway show in history
22 February 1983

Felix Hoffmann develops Aspirin
6 March 1899

David Marvin Jr sets human cannonball record
10 March 2011

Plastic wheelie bin invented
12 March 1968

Discovery of anti-matter
15 March 1962

World's first shopping mall opens in Michigan
22 March 1954

Werner Heisenberg publishes his Uncertainty Principle
23 March 1927

SOS distress signal developed
1 April 1905

The Beatles split up
10 April 1970

The most boring day in history according to one study
11 April 1954

Apple co-founder Ron Wayne sells 10% share for $800
12 April 1976

Patent filed for caller screening
8 May 1976

Patent filed for toilet brush
28 May 1933

First alarm clock with snooze feature
1 June 1959

Launch of the Doomsday Clock
2 June 1947

Museum of Failure opens in Sweden
7 June 2017

Domino's Pizza founded
10 June 1960

Donald Trump announces presidential run
16 June 2015

First International Potato Processing and Storage Convention
23 June 2009

Roy Sullivan struck by lightning for seventh time
25 June 1977

Release of *The Room*, directed by Tommy Wiseau, widely regarded as the worst film ever made
27 June 2003

Leopold Loyka, chauffeur to Archduke Ferdinand, makes wrong turn, encounters assassin and causes World War One
28 June 1914

999 emergency line launched in the UK
30 June 1937

Isaac Newton defines concept of inertia
5 July 1687

First lonely hearts ad
19 July 1695

Longest total solar eclipse of 21st century
22 July 2009

First self-checkout machine
5 August 1992

UK Bankruptcy Act
9 August 1869

32mm of rain falls in five minutes on Preston, UK
10 August 1893

Cricketer Don Bradman dismissed without score in final innings
14 August 1948

Potato chips invented
24 August 1853

World's largest turnip grown in USA
1 September 2004

Bon Accord lose 36–0 to Arbroath, the heaviest defeat in professional football
12 September 1885

First perforated toilet roll
15 September 1891

Battle of Karánsebes, in which the Austrian army accidentally fought itself and lost 10,000 men
21 September 1788

First edition of *Microwave for One* by Sonia Allison
23 September 1987

World record for most spoons balanced on face (31)
28 September 2013

Health and Safety at Work Act (UK)
1 October 1974

Fox News starts broadcasting
7 October 1996

World's largest cup of coffee (2,010 gallons) served in Las Vegas
15 October 2010

Black Monday
19 October 1987

First income tax laws introduced (USA)
22 October 1914

Beginning of the Great Depression
29 October 1929

M25 orbital road completed in UK
29 October 1986

First UK motorway services opens at Watford Gap
2 November 1959

Mary Celeste sets sail
7 November 1872

24-hour drinking laws introduced in UK
24 November 2005

John Michell predicts the existence of black holes
27 November 1783

Meteor strikes Ann Hodges, who survives with bruises
30 November 1954

Public launch of the Segway
3 December 2001

First Wetherspoon's pub opens
9 December 1979

Chris Rea's handwritten lyrics to 'Road to Hell' fail to sell at charity auction
15 December 2010

LinkedIn founded
28 December 2002

The Quantified Loser
Use this spread to keep track of the decline

	Jan	Feb	March	April	May	June
Weight gained						
Debt accumulated						
Falls/ grazes						
Aspirin taken						
Self-owns						
Public shamings						
Twitter blocks						
Arrests/ cautions						
Sleepless nights						
Duvet days						
Netflix hours						
Publisher rejections						
Tinder rejections						

July	Aug	Sept	Oct	Nov	Dec	Year-end total

Personal SWOT Analysis

Strengths

_____

_____

_____

_____

Weaknesses

_____

_____

_____

_____

_____

_____

_____

_____

_____

_____

_____

_____

_____

_____

_____

_____

_____

_____

_____

Opportunities
_____
_____
_____
_____
_____

Threats
_____
_____
_____
_____
_____
_____
_____
_____
_____
_____
_____
_____
_____
_____
_____
_____
_____
_____
_____
_____

What realistic and justifiable fears are stopping you achieving your goals?

28
LinkedIn founded, 2002
Debbie Reynolds, d.2016

29
Sam Peckinpah, d.1984

30
Bob Monkhouse, d.2003

31

1
Hank Williams, d.1953
Townes Van Zandt, d.1997
New Year's Day

2

3
Leonardo da Vinci unsuccessfully tests flying machine, 1496
Derek Acorah, d.2020

Write down three things in life for which you are grateful, not including travelators

4

5

Amelia Earhart, d.1939

6

7

8

9

10

David Bowie, d.2016

Name three simple steps someone
else could take to be healthier

11

12

13
James Joyce, d.1941

14
Cyrille Regis, d.2018

15
First automobile hearse in use, 1909

16

17
Shep, d.1987

If a genie granted you three wishes, how would you go about taking your revenge on the world?

18

19

20
Audrey Hepburn, d.1993

21
Black Monday, 2008
Terry Jones, d. 2020

22
Edvard Munch inspired to paint 'The Scream', 1892

23

24
First canned beer sold, 1935
Mark E. Smith, d.2018

Think about someone who once did you a small kindness. Ask them for a bigger favour.

25

Burns Night
Visitor falls down stairs in Fitzwilliam Museum, Cambridge, breaking three Qing Dynasty Chinese vases, 2006

26

First electric dental drill, 1875
Kobe Bryant, d.2020

27

Pete Seeger, d.2014

28

29

30

31

A.A. Milne, d.1956

If you were given one extra hour in every day, how much more could you drink?

1

2

3
Buddy Holly, d.1959

4
Facebook founded, 2004

5

6
First doughnut-making machine, 1926

7

Write down three pizza toppings that make you happy

8

9

10
Alexander Pushkin, d.1837

11
Sylvia Plath, d.1963

12

13

14
Valentine's Day

If you could change one thing about yourself, what five things would it be?

15

16
Longest traffic jam on record (109 miles), 1980

17

18

19
Harper Lee, d.2016

20

21
Duncan Edwards, d.1958

When was the last time you hurt someone's feelings – and what should they have learned from it?

FEBRUARY
Week 8

22
Opening and closing night of 'Moose Murders', worst-performing Broadway show in history, 1983

23
Stan Laurel, d.1965
Stanley Matthews, d.2000

24

25
Donald Bradman, d.2001

26

27

28

29
Leap. Year. Only.

If you had no fear, what could you do today – and how might it end badly?

1
St David's Day

2

3
Georges Perec, d.1982
Ivor Cutler, d.2006

4
John Candy, d.1994

5

6
Felix Hoffmann develops Aspirin, 1899
Mark Linkous, d.2010

7

What would your so-called best friend say is your biggest flaw?

8
International Women's Day

9

10
David Marvin Jr sets human cannonball record, 2011

11
Ken Dodd, d.2018

12
Plastic wheelie bin invented, 1968

13

14
Karl Marx, d.1883
Jim Bowen, d.2018
Stephen Hawking, d.2018

What job do you see yourself getting fired from in five years' time?

15
Discovery of anti-matter, 1962

16

17
St Patrick's Day

18
Chuck Berry, d.2017

19
Arthur C. Clarke, d.2008

20

21

If you found out you only had one day to live, roughly what time would you get up?

22
Johann Wolfgang von Goethe, d.1832
World's first shopping mall opens in Michigan, 1954

23
Werner Heisenberg publishes his Uncertainty Principle, 1927

24
Johan Cruyff, d.2016
Garry Shandling, d.2016

25

26

27
Ian Dury, d.2000

28
Virginia Woolf, d.1941

How would you describe yourself to an impressionable stranger?

29

30

31
Isaac Newton, d.1727
Jesse Owens, d.1980

1
April Fool's Day
SOS distress signal developed, 1905

2

3

4

What's the best piece of unsolicited advice you've ignored?

5
Kurt Cobain, d.1994

6

7
P.T. Barnum, d.1891

8
Frank Mars, d.1934
Pablo Picasso, d.1973

9
Edward Thomas, d.1917

10
The Beatles split up, 1970
Robert Edwards, d.2013

11
The most boring day in history according to one study, 1954

Who would play you in the fish-out-of-water crime-caper screwball-comedy TV movie of your life?

12

Franklin D. Roosevelt, d.1945
Apple co-founder Ron Wayne sells 10% share for $800, 1976

13

14

15

Thomas Andrews, d.1912
Greta Garbo, d.1990

16

17

Gabriel García Márquez, d.2014

18

Albert Einstein, d.1955
Anne Williams, d.2013

If you could talk to your younger self, what hand gestures would you use for emphasis?

19

Charles Darwin, d.1882
Levon Helm, d.2012

20

Rubin Carter, d.2014

21

Prince Rogers Nelson, d.2016

22

23

St George's Day

24

25

Saul Bass, d.1996

"I have not failed. I've just found 10,000 ways that won't work."

THOMAS EDISON ;)

26

27

28
Charley Patton, d.1934

29

30
Casey Jones, d.1900

1
Ayrton Senna, d.1994
International Workers' Day

2
Leonardo da Vinci, d.1519

"There are no traffic jams along the extra mile."

ROGER STAUBACH >.<

3

4
Adam Yauch, d.2012

5

6
Henry David Thoreau, d.1862

7

8
Patent filed for caller screening, 1976
Maurice Sendak, d.2012

9

"Nothing is impossible; the word itself says 'I'm possible'!"

AUDREY HEPBURN ¯_(ツ)_/¯

10

11
Bob Marley, d.1981
Douglas Adams, d.2001

12

13
Doris Day, d.2019

14
Frank Sinatra, d.1998

15
June Carter Cash, d.2003

16

"There is only one way to avoid criticism: do nothing, say nothing, and be nothing."

ARISTOTLE :)

17

18
Ian Curtis, d.1980

19

20

21

22
World Goth Day

23
Bonnie Parker, d.1934
Roger Moore, d.2017

"The best angle from which to approach any problem is the try-angle."

ANONYMOUS, UNDERSTANDABLY

24

25

26
Samuel Pepys, d.1703

27

28
Patent filed for toilet brush, 1933
Eric Morecambe, d.1984
John Noakes, d.2017

29

30
Christopher Marlowe, d.1593

"The only difference between try and triumph is a little umph."

ANONYMOUS, PROBABLY THE SAME GUY

31

1
First alarm clock with snooze feature, 1959

2
Launch of the Doomsday Clock, 1947

3
Muhammad Ali, d.2016

4
David Markson, d.2010

5
Ray Bradbury, d.2012

6

"Be thankful for what you have;
  you'll end up having more. If you
  concentrate on what you don't
  have, you will never, ever have
  enough."

OPRAH WINFREY, NET WORTH $2.7 BILLION

7

Alan Turing, d.1954
Dorothy Parker, d.1967
Museum of Failure opens in Sweden, 2017

8

Gerard Manley Hopkins, d.1889

9

Hovis Presley, d.2005

10

Domino's Pizza founded, 1960
Les Dawson, d.1993

11

12

13

"Great minds discuss ideas;
 average minds discuss events;
 small minds discuss people."

ELEANOR ROOSEVELT
(WHAT DO YOU THINK OF HER?)

14

15
Ella Fitzgerald, d.1996

16
Donald Trump announces presidential run, 2015

17

18

19
James Gandolfini, d.2013

20

"Pearls don't lie on the seashore. If you want one, you must dive for it."

ANCIENT UNHELPFUL PROVERB

21
Niccolò Machiavelli, d.1527

22
Judy Garland, d.1969

23
First International Potato Processing and Storage Convention, 2009

24

25
Roy Sullivan struck by lightning for seventh time, 1977
Michael Jackson, d.2009

26

27
Tove Jansson, d.2001
Release of 'The Room', directed by Tommy Wiseau, widely regarded as the worst film ever made, 2003

"Don't stop when you are tired. Stop when you are done."

BAD DRIVING ADVICE PROVERB

28
*Leopold Loyka, chauffeur to Archduke Ferdinand, makes wrong turn,
encounters assassin and causes World War One, 1914*

29

30
999 emergency line launched in the UK, 1937

1
Marlon Brando, d.2004

2
Ernest Hemingway, d.1961
Caroline Aherne, d.2016

3

4
Marie Curie, d.1934
Independence Day (USA)

"There are seven days in the week and 'someday' is not one of them."

5
Isaac Newton defines concept of inertia, 1687

6
Aneurin Bevan, d.1960

7

8

SOMEDAY

10

11

Don't worry, there's always a chance things will work out through sheer luck and random externalities. You got this.

12

13

14
Bastille Day (France)

15

16

17
Billie Holiday, d.1959
John Coltrane, d.1967

18
Caravaggio, d.1610

Fall seven times, stand up eight, go back to bed

19
First lonely hearts ad, 1695
Alan Lomax, d.2002

20

21

22
Longest total solar eclipse of 21st century, 2009

23
Amy Winehouse, d.2011

24

25
Samuel Taylor Coleridge, d.1834

You miss 100% of the shots you don't drink

26

27

28

29
Vincent van Gogh, d.1890

30

31
Bobby Robson, d.2009

1
Cilla Black, d.2015

If not now, then whenever

2

3

Joseph Conrad, d.1924
Lenny Bruce, d.1966

4

5

Marilyn Monroe, d.1962
First self-checkout machine, 1992
Barry Chuckle, d.2018

6

Francis Ponge, d.1988

7

8

If you can't beat them,
subtweet them

9

10
32mm of rain falls in five minutes on Preston, UK, 1893
Tony Wilson, d.2007

11
Robin Williams, d.2014

12
William Blake, d.1827

13

14
Cricketer Don Bradman dismissed without score in final innings, 1948

15

Crappe diem

16
Robert Johnson, d.1938
Aretha Franklin, d.2018

17

18
Bruce Forsyth, d.2017

19
Federico García Lorca, d.1936
Groucho Marx, d.1977

20
Jerry Lewis, d.2017

21

22

If a tree falls in the woods and no one is there to hear it, does that remind you of your life?

23

24
Potato chips invented, 1853

25
Neil Armstrong, d.2012
John McCain, d.2018

26

27

28

29
Gene Wilder, d.2016

Genius is 99% perspiration and you've mastered that bit

30
Seamus Heaney, d.2013

31

1
World's largest turnip grown in USA, 2004

2
J. R. R. Tolkien, d.1973

3

4
Steve Irwin, d.2006
Joan Rivers, d.2014

5

There's no business like your bad idea for a start-up business

---

6

7

8

9

10

11
Roko Camaj, d.2001

12
Bon Accord lose 36–0 to Arbroath, the heaviest defeat in professional football, 1885
Johnny Cash, d.2003

Another day, another net loss

13

14
Grace Kelly, d.1982

15
Isambard Kingdom Brunel, d.1859
First perforated toilet roll, 1891

16

17

18
Jimi Hendrix, d.1970

19

When the going gets tough, tough

20

21

Virgil, d.19BC
Battle of Karánsebes, in which the Austrian army accidentally fought itself and lost
10,000 men, 1788
Alan Fletcher, d.2006

22

23

First edition of 'Microwave for One' by Sonia Allison, 1987

24

25

26

Dance like nobody's pointing and laughing

27

28
Herman Melville, d.1891
World record for most spoons balanced on face (31), 2013

29
Bill Shankly, d.1981

30
James Dean, d.1955

1
Health and Safety at Work Act (UK), 1974

2
Tom Petty, d.2017

3
Woody Guthrie, d.1967
Peter Norman, d.2006

The darkest part of night is just before the dawn of another pointless day

---

4
Janis Joplin, d.1970

5
Steve Jobs, d.2011

6

7
Fox News starts broadcasting, 1996

8

9

10
Jack Daniel, d.1911
Orson Welles, d.1985

You make your own incredibly bad luck

11

12
Hispanic Day

13

14

15
World's largest cup of coffee (2,010 gallons) served in Las Vegas, 2010

16
Sean Hughes, d.2017

17

Every cloud has a silver lining
around its heavy grey mass of
imminent rain

18

Thomas Edison, d.1931

19

Black Monday, 1987

20

21

Jack Kerouac, d.1969

22

First income tax laws introduced (USA), 1914

23

24

Rosa Parks, d.2005
Fats Domino, d.2017

There are plenty more fish in the vast, implacable ocean

25
Geoffrey Chaucer, d.1400
John Peel, d.2004

26

27
Lou Reed, d.2013

28
Ted Hughes, d.1998

29
Beginning of the Great Depression, 1929
M25 orbital road completed in UK, 1986

30

31
Hallowe'en

What doesn't kill you makes you wish it had

1
Ezra Pound, d.1972

2
First UK motorway services opens at Watford Gap, 1959

3
Ernst Gombrich, d.2001

4

5
Jacques Tati, d.1982
Bonfire Night

6

7
'Mary Celeste' sets sail, 1872
Steve McQueen, d.1980
Leonard Cohen, d.2016

Everything happens for a terrifyingly random reason

8

John Milton, d.1674

9

10

Arthur Rimbaud, d.1891

11

George Edwin Ellison, d.1918

12

13

14

If at first you don't succeed,
get used to it

15

16

17

18

19

20

21

You can run but you are better at hiding

22

John F. Kennedy, d.1963

23

24

24-hour drinking laws introduced in UK, 2005
Clive James, d.2019

25

26

27

Horace, d.8BC
John Michell predicts the existence of black holes, 1783

28

When one door closes, another one opens in your face

NOVEMBER / DECEMBER
Week 48

29
George Harrison, d.2001

30
Oscar Wilde, d.1900
Meteor strikes Ann Hodges, who survives with bruises, 1954
St Andrew's Day

1

2
Odetta, d.2008

3
Public launch of the Segway, 2001

4
Frank Zappa, d.1993
Bob Willis, d.2019

5
Wolfgang Amadeus Mozart, d.1791
Nelson Mandela, d.2013

Personal injury insurance is the best policy

6

7

8
John Lennon, d.1980

9
First Wetherspoon's pub opens, 1979
Patrick Moore, d.2012

10
Otis Redding, d.1967
Richard Pryor, d.2005

11
Sam Cooke, d.1964
Keith Chegwin, d.2017

12

Red sky at night, something's not right. Red sky in the morning, lingering feeling something terrible is going to happen.

13

14

15
Walt Disney, d.1966
Chris Rea's handwritten lyrics to 'Road to Hell' fail to sell at charity auction, 2010

16

17

18
Kirsty MacColl, d.2000

19

Deck the halls with melancholy

20
John Steinbeck, d.1968

21

22
Joe Strummer, d.2002

23

24
William Thackeray, d.1863

25
Charlie Chaplin, d.1977
Dean Martin, d.1995
George Michael, d.2016
Christmas Day

26

Same shit, different year

27
Carrie Fisher, d.2016

28
LinkedIn founded, 2002
Debbie Reynolds, d.2016

29
Sam Peckinpah, d.1984

30
Bob Monkhouse, d.2003

31

1
Hank Williams, d.1953
Townes Van Zandt, d.1997
New Year's Day

2

The Gaping Void Ahead
Next Year Planner

January

February

March

April

May

June

The Gaping Void Ahead
Next Year Planner

July

August

September

October

November

December

People Who Never Call

Name

Address

Telephone

Mobile

Email

Name

Address

Telephone

Mobile

Email

Name

Address

Telephone

Mobile

Email

Name

Address

Telephone

Mobile

Email

Name

Address

Telephone

Mobile

Email

Name

Address

Telephone

Mobile

Email

People You Owe Money

Name   Amount
Address

Telephone
Mobile
Email

Name   Amount
Address

Telephone
Mobile
Email

Name   Amount
Address

Telephone
Mobile
Email

Name   Amount

Address

Telephone

Mobile

Email

Name   Amount

Address

Telephone

Mobile

Email

Name   Amount

Address

Telephone

Mobile

Email

Imaginary Friends

Name

Address

Telephone

Mobile

Email

Name

Address

Telephone

Mobile

Email

Name

Address

Telephone

Mobile

Email

Name

Address

Telephone

Mobile

Email

Name

Address

Telephone

Mobile

Email

Name

Address

Telephone

Mobile

Email

Real Enemies

Name
Address

Telephone
Mobile
Email

Name
Address

Telephone
Mobile
Email

Name
Address

Telephone
Mobile
Email

Name

Address

Telephone

Mobile

Email

Name

Address

Telephone

Mobile

Email

Name

Address

Telephone

Mobile

Email

Notes Toward A Dull Novel

Notes Toward A Laboured Poem

Notes Toward An
Abandoned Screenplay

Notes Toward An
Incomplete Haiku

Notes Toward A Tweet
Everyone Will Ignore

Notes From A Boring Meeting

Notes From An Urgent
Performance Appraisal

Ideas You'll Never Follow Up

Laughable To-Do List

Apology Notes

Dear

I'm incredibly sorry for

From

Dear

I'm incredibly sorry for

From

Dear

I'm incredibly sorry for

From

Dear

I'm incredibly sorry for

From

Dear

I'm incredibly sorry for

From

Dear

I'm incredibly sorry for

From

Passive-Aggressive Notes

Dear
Just so you know,

Have a great day.
From

Dear
Just so you know,

Have a great day.
From

Dear
Just so you know,

Have a great day.
From

Dear

Just so you know,

Have a great day.

From

Dear

Just so you know,

Have a great day.

From

Dear

Just so you know,

Have a great day.

From

Boring Crossword

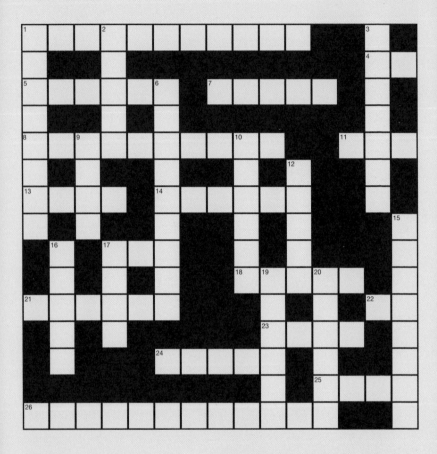

ACROSS

1 Frusrtation (anag) (11)
4 To hell with … (2)
5 Root vegetable (6)
7 Leave me … (5)
8 The what of the long distance runner (10)
11 I'm sorry I ran over your … (3)
13 I will pay you back another … (4)
14 I need to go to the … (6)
17 A nice … down (3)
18 I thought it was fancy … (5)
21 More than one pizza (6)
22 Are you enjoying this crossword? (2)
23 Grim but with lu instead of ri (4)
24 One who loses (5)
25 Type of deficiency you definitely have in your diet (4)
26 Your parents are what in you (12)

DOWN

1 Utility with an 'f' (8)
2 You lack a … of purpose (5)
3 I'm sorry I made a … (7)
6 If something has no point, it is … (9)
9 Sounds like dumb but starts with 'n' (4)
10 Must you talk … … ? (2–4)
12 Thousand-yard … (5)
15 Anagrams are anoyning (8)
16 Itoid (anag) (5)
17 Get it yourself, you … bastard (4)
19 The egret has an 'r'? (6)
20 Rhymes with Cupid and starts with 'st' (6)

Misspelt Wordsearch

```
P T S A I G M W Y N J C T T S
R R O C S G I I J M E I N U D
I U T C D E N E S M I E Q I Q
B N A I R Y U O A S M H S S S
S T T D H P L T R R P A Z E S
O I O E Q A E E E E S E S P E
D L P N L R O V T T N A L E N
Q L U T Y L O R E A U C K R E
U L Q A J G I R A C N I E A K
R R H L R K O G E H C I W T N
H I L Y S U V B A M P S F E U
C J E D S J Z H I N Q A C E R
I L E E X I S T A N C E W O D
G N I S S A R A B M E E O Y J
E V E I C E R V A C C U U M S
```

ACCIDENTALY   GOVERMENT   UNTILL
BECUASE   IGNORENCE   VACCUUM
CEMATERY   INTELLIGANCE   WICH
DEFINATELY   MISSPEL   WIERD
DISASTEROUS   PHAROAH
DRUNKENESS   POTATOS
EMBARASSING   RECIEVE
EXISTANCE   SEPERATE

Bleak Strategies

A series of unhelpful prompts for overcoming creative blocks. Cut them out and select randomly.

BE YOUR DOUBTS

FEAR CHANGE

BREATHE FASTER

HIDE FROM THE PROBLEM

PERSONALISE THE ISSUE

QUESTION THE GOOD THINGS

INTERNALISE YOUR ANGER

OVERANALYSE PEOPLE'S INTENTIONS

CHECK SOCIAL MEDIA

ESCALATE THE ARGUMENT

ABANDON THE PROJECT

SLEEP ON IT

Excuse Generator

Use this flow chart to get out of whatever it is now

I can't give you a lift to the airport	I can't come to your party	I didn't bring a gift
I can't make your book launch		I forgot your birthday
I did not listen to your podcast	I missed the funeral	I can't pay you back right now
I can't come in today	I drove through the red light	I can't talk right now

BECAUSE

I am under house arrest	it was / is / will be raining	I am / was / will be drunk
of all the charitable work I do		I literally have no money
my dog died. I bought it recently. Winston. Car accident.	nothing matters	of the government
of the voices	my cat died. I bought it recently. Simba. Diabetes.	*bursts into tears*

Even-Worse-Case Scenarios

Survival advice for slightly more extreme situations.
Do not follow this advice.

ESCAPING QUICKSAND WITH A HANGOVER

If you're ankle deep or knee deep in quicksand after a heavy night, slowly sit down and raise one hand to bystanders to indicate the need to keep the noise down. If you're waist deep, lie flat on your back, close your eyes, pinch the bridge of your nose between your thumb and middle finger, breathe out and wait quietly for assistance.

SURVIVING AN ELEPHANT STAMPEDE WHILE RUNNING INTO AN EX

Where possible, climb or hide behind a tree without looking like you're trying to avoid your ex. If your ex takes cover in the same place, keep conversation short and light – don't rehash the past or try to justify your life, and lie down as elephants typically avoid stepping on a prone human being. If the elephant returns to the spot, play dead and don't look for closure.

FIGHTING A CROCODILE WHILE TIRED

Don't try to keep its mouth open with your hands – a crocodile's jaws close with the force of 13 tons per square inch and you hardly slept last night. A crocodile's skin is too thick to pierce and its head is a solid mass of bone, the same way yours feels right now. Try poking your fingers into its eyes and aim to get more vitamin D into your diet.

NEGOTIATING WITH A HOSTAGE-TAKER WHOSE NAME YOU HAVE TEMPORARILY FORGOTTEN

If you have established the hostage-taker's name earlier in the conversation but are now drawing a blank, gently steer the conversation towards specific demands. While avoiding terms of direct consent or refusal, try to get the hostage-taker to see the demands as unfeasible and ask him how he's spelling his name. Keep him talking and, if the name comes back to you, mentally associate it with something pictorial like a cartoon character.

JUMPING FROM A MOVING VEHICLE WITH HAYFEVER

At a speed of 35mph you will travel 250 yards between jumping and hitting the ground. Look well ahead for a soft spot on which to land, but avoid recently mown verges. Open the door firmly, lean your upper body outwards, clasp your hands behind your head and jump towards the back of the vehicle to meet the ground in a rolling motion. Avoid jumping when the air is warming up and cooling down as pollen count is highest at these times – around 8–10 a.m. and 5–7 p.m.

PERFORMING THE HEIMLICH MANOEUVRE ON A FIRST DATE

Ask 'Are you choking?' and always remember to listen and sound interested. If your date is unable to speak, position yourself behind them and reach your arms around their waist – being tactile helps to establish intimacy and is vital to performing abdominal thrusts. Place your fist, thumb-side in, just above your date's belly button, grasp the fist tightly with your other hand, and make sharp upward thrusts. However intense things get, avoid saying 'I love you'.

Unhelpful Folk Rhymes

The rhyme-as-reason effect suggests people are more likely to believe advice when it rhymes. Do not follow the advice in these rhymes.

WINTER DRIVING

When the snow falls hard, brake harder still
and high is the gear that descends the hill

LEAP YEAR

If the year divides itself by three
a leap year it shall surely be

CLOCKS

Spring *back* in fright
Fall *forward* from a height

DRUNKEN EMAILS

Drunken emails
charm the females

RECOVERY POSITION

If a pal's unconscious and it's all gone south
keep their legs apart and their thumb in their mouth

CAMPFIRES

You get more heat
when the ground is peat

WIRING (UK)

Blue is the Earth revolving round
and neutral comes in deepest brown
but the livest wire you've ever seen
is the yellow and the green

WORKPLACE SAFETY

Asbestos ... is best boss!

SUSPICIOUS PACKAGES

See it. Say it. Sit on it.

REMEMBER

Remember, remember
the eighth of September

MUSHROOMS

The more suspicious
the more delicious

EMERGENCY STOP

Into neutral, steer hard right
Handbrake, mirror, signal, lights

GOOD LUCK

See a dead cat, pick it up
All day long you'll have good luck

Pointless Doodles

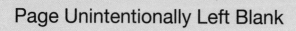
Page Unintentionally Left Blank

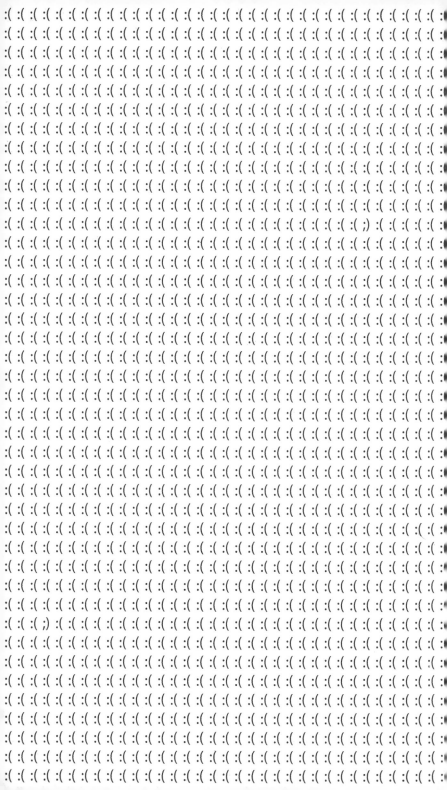